Electronic Surveillance of Mobile Devices

Understanding the Mobile Ecosystem and Applicable Surveillance Law

Edward Balkovich, Don Prosnitz, Anne Boustead, Steven C. Isley

For more information on this publication, visit www.rand.org/t/RR800

This project was supported by Award No. 2011-IJ-CX-K058, awarded by the National Institute of Justice, Office of Justice Programs, U.S. Department of Justice. The opinions, findings, and conclusions or recommendations expressed in this publication are those of the authors and do not necessarily reflect those of the Department of Justice.

Library of Congress Control Number: 2015959716
ISBN: 978-0-8330-9242-7

Support RAND
Make a tax-deductible charitable contribution at
www.rand.org/giving/contribute

www.rand.org

Preface

Mobile phones, the networks they connect to, the applications they use, and the services they access all collect and retain enormous amounts of information that can be useful in criminal investigations. However, consumer use of encryption and other information security practices has also grown. While encryption serves many important functions, it also may leave law enforcement unable to access information during criminal investigations, even when they have sought and received appropriate legal permission. The simultaneous increase in both consumer information and barriers to accessing that information has lead to a debate about whether we are entering a "golden age of surveillance" or an age in which electronic surveillance will "go dark."

Our goal was to create a tool that could help law enforcement, policymakers, and privacy advocates understand both what information is available in the mobile ecosystem and how law enforcement may be able to access this information. State and local law enforcement face two substantial challenges when accessing these data. The first is maintaining awareness of the sources and nature of commercial data available to an investigator; law enforcement may be overlooking helpful information because officers are simply unaware of its existence. The second is determining the legal rules for access to these data, since there is often uncertainty about how to interpret existing surveillance law with respect to mobile technology.

This report is the first of two documents describing an electronic surveillance study sponsored by the National Institute of Justice. This first volume discusses the challenges outlined above and describes the development of a prototype tool—the Mobile Information and Knowledge Ecosystem (MIKE)—intended to help law enforcement, commercial entities, and policy analysts explore the mobile ecosystem and understand the laws regulating law enforcement's use of data contained within the mobile ecosystem. The tool might also serve as a mechanism for sharing best practices in electronic surveillance. This report should be of interest to decisionmakers in law enforcement, the commercial sector, government, and public advocacy groups interested in electronic surveillance, public safety, and privacy.

This report is written for a nontechnical audience. A forthcoming companion document, *A Guide to the Structure and Intended Use of MIKE*, written for practitioners interested in using our tool, describes the prototype that we developed. It explains the tool's principles, illustrates its potential uses, and describes how to add content.

The RAND Justice Policy Program

The research reported here was conducted in the RAND Justice Policy Program, which spans both criminal and civil justice systems issues, with topics including public safety, effective policing, police-community relations, drug policy and enforcement, corrections policy, use of technology in law enforcement, tort reform, catastrophe and mass injury compensation, court resourcing, and insurance regulation. Program research is supported by government agencies, foundations, and the private sector.

This program is part of RAND Justice, Infrastructure, and Environment, a division of the RAND Corporation dedicated to improving policy and decisionmaking in a wide range of policy domains, including civil and criminal justice, infrastructure protection and homeland security, transportation and energy policy, and environmental and natural resource policy.

Questions or comments about this report should be sent to the project leader, Ed Balkovich (edwardb@rand.org). For more information about the Justice Policy Program, see http://www.rand.org/jie or contact the director at justice@rand.org.

Contents

Figures and Tables

Figures

Tables

Summary

Mobile phones are pervasive—virtually everyone today carries a cell phone, most of which are smartphones. There are powerful economic incentives for commercial entities in the mobile ecosystem to collect and retain very detailed data about users. As a result, mobile phones, the networks they connect to, the applications they use, and the services they access all collect and retain enormous amounts of information that can be useful in criminal investigations. Access to these data is subject to a patchwork of rules, creating a complicated environment within which law enforcement must operate.

Law enforcement officers face several important challenges to finding and using the trove of information in the mobile ecosystem: The types of information available and methods of obtaining it change with quickly evolving technology and commercial relationships, the law governing commercial information sharing is complex and uncertain, and countermeasures to evade surveillance are increasingly available. Because of these challenges, law enforcement officers may not make optimal decisions about whether and how to use mobile data. Officers may be unaware of what information exists and which commercial entities control information of interest. Due to legal complexity, they may either unnecessarily constrain themselves and risk public safety, or they may overreach and potentially violate civil liberties. Law enforcement access to information from the mobile ecosystem also poses challenges to commercial entities, who must determine how to respond to an increasing number of government information requests. Finally, policymakers are challenged to determine how to regulate the complex and opaque web of technologies and business relationships.

To help overcome these challenges, we developed and prototyped a tool—the Mobile Information and Knowledge Ecosystem (MIKE)—that functions like a map to help a wide range of stakeholders understand how information is shared within the mobile ecosystem, and the legal protections that govern access to that information. MIKE was constructed using semantic mediawiki, an extension to the software used to operate Wikipedia, resulting in a tool which is easy and intuitive to use. MIKE is interactive and designed so that new information can be added by users, thus maintaining the currency of the information—an essential characteristic, given the rapid change in mobile technology. Using MIKE, law enforcement, commercial entities, and policy analysts can provide, navigate, and analyze technical, commercial, and legal information related to electronic surveillance.

Preliminary assessments of this prototype and its potential uses from representatives of these stakeholder communities suggest that our approach has utility in all three domains. After seeing our approach and tool, a sample of stakeholders from the law enforcement community, industry, and policy advocacy groups judged our tool as a potentially useful way to explore the mobile ecosystem and understand the laws regulating law enforcement's use of data contained within the mobile ecosystem, as well as a possible mechanism for sharing best practices in electronic surveillance. Going forward, a key question is how much information in the tool to make publicly available, and a key concern is how such a potentially valuable tool could be sustained.

This report briefly outlines our work on the development of an electronic surveillance ecosystem tool. Chapter One describes the challenges posed by electronic surveillance in an age of mobile devices. In Chapter Two, we discuss our goals and objectives in meeting that challenge and how we derived these objectives. In Chapter Three, we explain how we developed a software tool to meet these goals and objectives. MIKE is introduced and described in Chapter Four. Chapter Five discusses stakeholders' initial assessment of this tool. Finally, in Chapter Six, we address perhaps the most critical issue—sustainment—by identifying a number of plausible options for keeping the tool relevant and up to date. A consideration for future research would be to analyze these options and identify a sustainment approach that will support further development of the prototype.

Acknowledgments

The authors want to thank a number of people that helped us with this project. First is our colleague Karlyn Stanley. A number of law enforcement partners assisted us as expert advisors about the conduct of investigations and use of electronic surveillance. They included representatives of the District of Columbia Metropolitan Police Department, the Indiana State Police, and the Las Vegas Metropolitan Police Department. In addition, a number of individuals helped us to understand commercial concerns and perspectives and the perspectives of policy analysts, advocates, and decisionmakers active in this area. We would also like to thank our reviewers, Lily Ablon (RAND Corporation) and James Dempsey (University of California, Berkeley, School of Law), for their helpful comments and feedback.

CHAPTER ONE

The Electronic Surveillance Challenge

This project was motivated by the changing relationship between mobile technology and law enforcement. Therefore, in order to fully address issues related to government access to information derived from the mobile ecosystem, our definition of electronic surveillance is deliberately and necessarily broad. We include law enforcement use of active investigative techniques to intercept and record information, such as the use of wiretaps and interceptions of communications. However, in contrast to the definitions of electronic surveillance utilized in other contexts, we also include law enforcement use of information recorded and collected by commercial entities, such as location records generated through use of a mobile device.[1] This broad definition of electronic surveillance is used in order to provide law enforcement with a more complete picture of how it can interact with the mobile ecosystem, and to fully explore the policy issues created by this interaction.

Electronic surveillance is a valuable tool for law enforcement. It can improve public safety, guide criminal investigations, and provide compelling evidence in a prosecution. State and local law enforcement officials are well aware of the value of data generated by mobile devices. They are also becoming aware that a particular type of data may be available from multiple sources. For example, information may be col-

---

[1]   A narrower interpretation, analogous to that used in many legal contexts, would interpret these differently. The former would be considered surveillance; the latter would be considered data given to a third party. In practice, advertising-driven services and apps collect both metadata and content, and it is useful to conceptualize it as a form of commercial surveillance.

lected and stored by the device itself, the network on which the device operates, and the many services[2] and applications[3] accessed through the device. Collectively, device makers, network operators, and app developers, among numerous other entities, make up what Silicon Valley refers to as the *mobile ecosystem.* Though information obtained through electronic surveillance is enormously valuable, law enforcement professionals also understand that surveillance can be invasive and must be conducted in a legal framework intended to protect privacy and civil liberties. Technological, commercial, and legal trends make balancing these equities a significant challenge for both law enforcement and the broader policy community.

Mobile Devices Changed Everything

The public has embraced mobile devices. The Wireless Association (CTIA—The Wireless Association, 2013) estimates that the number of mobile phones is comparable to the size of the U.S. population (326 million subscriptions at the end of 2012). Moreover, according to some estimates (Smith, 2012) more than half of these mobile devices are now smartphones or tablets, which are being used not only for communication, but also to access Internet-based services and conduct a wide range of transactions. The use of these services generates information revealing a person's whereabouts, relationships, and activities. Thus, it is increasingly likely that the subject of a criminal investigation or a public safety response will be carrying a mobile device that stores and generates information useful to law enforcement or public safety officials.

---

[2]   A *service* is a mechanism requiring interactions with computers other than the mobile phone that allows the user to undertake an activity. For example, Tor is a service that allows the user to conduct activities on the Internet anonymously. Services are typically accessed via a browser or an app.

[3]   A *mobile application*, or app, is a piece of software that runs on a mobile operating system and allows the user to perform an activity. For example, RunKeeper is an application that allows the user to track his or her athletic activity.

In the mid-2000s, Wireless Association estimates showed that the Short Message Service (SMS) was displacing voice service. Now, it appears that SMS is in turn being overtaken by the use of app-based communication tools. Some industry observers (Sharma, 2013) note that apps such as WhatsApp[4]—a "free" Internet messaging application—now transmit more messages worldwide than *all* carriers' SMS services combined. The apps available for download to a mobile device number in the millions (Cocotas, 2013). Meeker (2014) estimates that mobile data traffic was 25 percent of all web usage in 2014 and growing at 14 percent year over year. These apps can be used for more than just communications. For example, while estimates of mobile financial transactions in 2013–2014 vary widely—ranging between $12 billion (Rolfe, 2014) and $235 billion (Statista, 2014)—they are clearly growing. Some estimates suggest the volume could be $1 trillion in 2017 (SwitchPay, 2014).

Taken together, these trends—the growth in data usage and transactions, and the displacement of SMS and voice—indicate that most of the services accessed with mobile devices will be implemented using Internet protocol (IP)-based protocols.[5] These trends mean that

---

[4]   WhatsApp is an Internet text and voice messaging service (WhatsApp, no date).

[5]   IP-based protocols can be used to provide services very similar to those provided by traditional telecommunication technologies. For example, Voice over IP (VoIP) uses packet switching. There is no concept of a "circuit" dedicated to the phone call, as there is in conventional Time Division Multiplexed telephony services. A conversation is broken into a sequence of packets, sent along potentially different paths through the network, and reassembled into the original sequence at the receiving phone. If no one is talking, then no packets are sent, and IP network resources are used for other purposes.

This new technology can be implemented in different ways, complicating law enforcement access to information. Two principal approaches to VoIP have emerged: carrier-grade and "over the top" (OTT). In a carrier-grade solution, the IP network provider is responsible for setting up, carrying, and tearing down the call. The phone is known to the carrier, and the carrier associates an IP address with the phone number assigned to that device. The call setup/tear down and conversation occur as a sequence of IP packets sent/received over the IP network also provided by the carrier. The carrier is in a position to tell when a call was made, what number was dialed, what was said, and when the call was terminated. The carrier is also in a position to make a copy of the packets generated by the call and send them to law enforcement.

OTT is an application (e.g., Skype or Vonage) installed on a smartphone or computer. It is not operated by the carrier providing Internet services. The carrier cannot determine what

traditional telecommunication carriers are no longer the exclusive or a comprehensive source of the kinds of information that a criminal investigator may seek. Investigators will increasingly want to go the app and service providers, many of which may well be small commercial entities with less experience working with law enforcement, for data valuable to their investigations. It is therefore unsurprising that requests for metadata and stored content appear to be growing dramatically, particularly when compared with more traditional forms of surveillance (Figure 1.1).[6] Awareness of these apps and services is critical for investigators.

With mobile devices, there are much more data available—not only phone numbers but also information on location, contacts, and financial transactions, for example. More significantly, the data may now be more accessible: stored both on the device itself and on the servers of the entities that the device communicates with. As device capacity increases, so does the amount of user data stored on the device.[7] Even continuous, real-time data—such as location information collected by a traffic-management app—may be retained indefinitely in multiple locations, confusing the previous clear distinction between real-time interception and stored information held by third parties.

However, there are countervailing trends that complicate law enforcement access to the mobile ecosystem. In particular, accompanying the growth in data is the growth of countermeasures—such as

---

is done with the packets sent via its broadband connection, without deep packet inspection. This is hard and expensive to do, and may be impossible if the user employs encryption. Thus, the application provider is the entity that becomes responsible for setting up and tearing down the call. If law enforcement knows that an individual is using Skype, it could present a warrant to Microsoft and expect them to perform the wiretap. An obvious countermeasure is to use multiple OTT VoIP apps.

[6]   Since there is no federal public reporting requirement of orders for metadata and stored content, the transparency reports of service providers assist as a proxy.

[7]   The Supreme Court has taken note of the special nature of cell phones, and the breadth and depth of information that may be contained on them. According to Chief Justice John Roberts, "[o]ne of the most notable distinguishing features of modern cell phones is their immense storage capacity," which allows the user to carry around extensive information about their activities." *Riley v. California*, 134 S. Ct. 2473, 2489 (2014).

Figure 1.1
Requests for Data from a Single Service Provider (Google) Outpace
Requests for Traditional Wiretaps

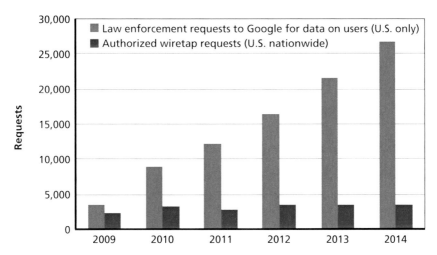

SOURCES: U.S. Courts Wiretap Reports and Google Transparency Reports (United States).

RAND RR800-1.1

encryption and onion routing[8]—which help individuals successfully hide information from electronic surveillance. There are many compelling social reasons for these privacy-enhancing technologies, including the protection of sensitive information and the encouragement of open speech by marginalized groups (Romanosky et al., 2015). However, the ready availability of these technologies and the decision of some commercial entities to implement them as defaults[9] have led some law enforcement agencies to claim that their existing surveillance methods are "going dark" and may no longer be useful in criminal investigations (Caproni, 2011; Comey, 2014).

---

[8]   Onion routing is a technique to hide the source and destination of a message over a network (Camenisch and Lysyanskaya, 2005).

[9]   This trend has predominantly occurred after the Snowdon revelations revealed the extent of government access to commercially collected data (Van Hoboken, 2013).

Law Enforcement Challenges

It almost goes without saying that the explosion of mobile devices has increased the storing and sharing of data that could be valuable to criminal investigations. More mobile devices, apps, and services mean more and richer data are available. Large service providers such as Google accumulate previously unimaginable amounts of metadata and stored content. More day-to-day activities are happening online than ever before, and data describing such activities are captured for commercial purposes. But state and local law enforcement face two substantial challenges when accessing these data.

The first challenge is *maintaining awareness of the sources and nature of commercial data* available to an investigator. Law enforcement may be overlooking helpful information because officers are simply unaware of its existence. In order to know what information is available, it is necessary to understand both the capabilities of the technology and the business practices of the commercial actors collecting useful data. However, the mobile ecosystem is developing rapidly, from both a technological and commercial perspective. Therefore, information about the carriers, apps, and services for mobile devices needs to be curated and organized for it to be useful by law enforcement in maintaining awareness and helping determine the best source of surveillance data needed for public safety and criminal investigations.

The second challenge is *determining the legal rules for access to these data*. As the kinds of electronic data collected by mobile technology grow richer, the number of service providers proliferates, and business models evolve, it becomes more challenging to identify with certainty the legal guidelines governing law enforcement's ability to lawfully obtain and use such data. An individual targeted by electronic surveillance is almost certainly mobile. The devices used by the target can run any of over a million apps and access a multitude of services—all of which capture new kinds of data and may span jurisdictional boundaries. But the legal constraints governing the use of and access to these data are evolving more slowly than the technology. These factors combine to create uncertainty about how to interpret existing surveillance law with respect to mobile technology—raising questions such as when a search warrant is needed and from whom it must be obtained.

False Dichotomies

Two false dichotomies must be avoided in this discussion. First, the debate between "going dark" and the "golden age of surveillance" is misleading. It is not a matter of one or the other; both conditions can exist at the same time. Technology has enabled the explosive growth of data generation and collection and the rise of privacy-enhancing technologies. Whether this leads to more or less effective surveillance depends primarily on the sophistication of the criminal and the nature of the crime, not policy and law. A sophisticated criminal executing a premeditated crime likely benefits from mobile technology that leaves law enforcement in the dark. A less savvy criminal or one committing a non-premeditated crime likely leaves behind a wealth of data previously unobtainable by law enforcement, creating a golden age of surveillance. Arguments for broad policy changes based on one or the other should be viewed with suspicion. Furthermore, future technology changes will have the potential to alter both of these conditions by either enabling the commercial collection of more personal data, or by denying access to it through privacy-enhancing services.

The alleged conflict between public safety and privacy is also a false dichotomy. It should not be a question of which one to protect, but rather how to craft policies that protect them both, because the information gathered by mobile technology is too important to both law enforcement and individuals. At the same time, the law enforcement community recognizes the importance of privacy protections and the privacy issues raised by electronic surveillance in the mobile technology. Policy advocates recognize the beneficial role that electronic surveillance can play in providing for public safety. These stakeholders are likely to be accepting of reasonable policies that balance these interests, particularly if the policy reduces uncertainty.

CHAPTER TWO

Our Project Was Designed to Meet the Needs of Key Stakeholders

Concern about government access to information contained within the mobile ecosystem is not limited to the law enforcement community. Thus, we formulated our project's objectives by considering the interests of a broad group of stakeholders. In particular, we were concerned with the implications of mobile technology for commerce, law enforcement, crime, law and jurisprudence, and public policy. Our aim was to create a tool that would recognize these implications and be beneficial to stakeholders in law enforcement, industry, and public policy. In this chapter, we describe the interests of various stakeholder groups implicated by law enforcement surveillance of the mobile ecosystem. We conclude this chapter by describing the objectives derived through this analysis.

Commercial Implications

Information contained in mobile devices and applications is important to the business community in developing advertising that is targeted to consumer interests and delivered via the same mobile devices from which personalized information about prospective customers is obtained.

A mobile device, its apps, and the services accessed from the device can all collect information about the user, including

- location, at varying frequencies and resolutions

- personal data, such as address books, contacts and acquaintances, and calendars
- communications, such as call and text details, and voice and text messages
- transactions, such as search queries and purchases
- photographs.

Such data are often collected by apps and services in order to fulfill their particular function. For example, a dining app must know your location in order to tell you what restaurants you are near. But data are also collected for other purposes, such as for use in developing ads that are tailored to the interests of the mobile user. Although assurances of anonymity are often provided to the user, it is possible in many cases to identify the user by linking together information obtained from a variety of sources (such as zip codes or dates of birth).[1]

Targeted advertising is the primary revenue model for many mobile apps and services—even when the app or service is licensed or sold (to generate revenue). A host of commercial entities mediate (behind the scenes) between mobile apps and services (Turow, 2011). These entities function as data brokers and market makers for advertising—collecting, processing, and selling information about mobile devices, apps, and services. These very complex and difficult-to-understand commercial relationships define the mobile ecosystem (see Appendix B).

---

[1]   Sweeney (2002) is often cited for recognizing the re-identification problem and illustrating several ways to re-identify individuals from data sets thought to be anonymous. It is also relatively easy to identify individuals from location data (de Montjoye et al., 2013). Turow (2011) describes how all of this makes it possible to target advertising to an individual. Re-identification is a particularly pressing problem when an ostensibly anonymous dataset can be related to an identified dataset. For example, Narayanan and Shmatikov (2008) suggest that it is possible to de-anonymize Netflix data by comparing those data with public ratings from the Internet Movie Database. They determined that "[i]n many cases, even a handful of movies that are rated by a subscriber in both services would be sufficient to identify his or her record in the Netflix Prize dataset (if present among the released records) with enough statistical confidence to rule out the possibility of a false match except for negligible probability" (p. 12).

The growing number of alternative sources of a single type of information can be appreciated by reflecting on how many of these apps, mediating entities, and services are in a position to collect, buy or sell, retain, combine, and analyze information about the user of a mobile device, and have the financial motivation to do so. Location information, for example, is collected and used by the carriers, by navigation and traffic management apps, and even by games such as *Angry Birds*. Thus, the same type of data may be available from multiple sources, depending on what apps are on a subject's mobile device.[2] The user specificity that these systems are beginning to achieve is precisely the type of specificity sought during a criminal investigation.

While the app or service may be visible to the user and law enforcement, the information brokers—intermediaries that make sophisticated advertising possible—operate largely out of public and law enforcement's view. Law enforcement and policy analysts need a way to identify who these information brokers are and to be aware of the alternative sources of electronic surveillance data, the privacy protections relevant to these sources of data, the legal processes needed to assess the information, and the need for and implications of policy changes.

Law Enforcement Implications

The previous chapter described how the use of mobile devices has changed the nature of electronic surveillance. Law enforcement no longer needs to cause surveillance data to be collected and retained—such as by ordering a wiretap.[3] Instead, surveillance data—content and metadata—are now pervasively collected and retained by commercial firms for their own purposes. Law enforcement need only obtain per-

---

[2]   Information about installed apps can be discovered from app stores, such as those operated by Apple and Google, because these stores retain the history of apps that a user has downloaded. Antivirus and malware protection apps also collect these data.

[3]   It is in the mobile ecosystem's financial interest to collect and use data about the users of mobile devices, apps and services. Mobile data are generally not ephemeral (as voice conversations were), but the commercial retention periods of such data vary.

mission to lawfully access these retained data to conduct surveillance. However, there are significant obstacles to lawful access.

The myriad and complex relationships between commercial entities collecting data from mobile devices, apps, and services are often opaque, making it difficult for law enforcement to be fully aware of the alternatives for surveillance data. Of course, ephemeral data (such as a conversations) remain an exception.[4] Commercial firms will not retain information that does not have commercial value, that is protected by legislation (e.g., the Child Online Privacy and Protection Act, which precludes collection of data from minors), or that is not needed to implement a service. But commercial entities have powerful economic incentives to collect, retain, and analyze data about users. When commercial data are collected, law enforcement has strong interests in the retention of that data and the ability to access it in a timely manner. Destruction of information or inability to access it in a timely manner can seriously impede an investigation—especially a multistep investigation.

There are several ways to identify the type of data collected through mobile technology. Apps and services typically publish privacy statements. These statements, while often vague, convoluted, and difficult to read, describe the kinds of data an app or service may access and how that data may be used and shared. More precise information can be obtained from the permissions that an app requests or by collecting and monitoring what data a device transmits when an app is active.

Consumers are aware of these commercial collection activities only if they read privacy statements or are asked to give an app permission to access specific types of data, such as location, calendars, and contacts. Unless the device user has an appreciation for the mobile ecosystem, the privacy implications of such requests are not obvious or easily understood. Likewise, without a rich understanding about apps

---

[4]   Notionally, both conventional and VoIP telephony services offer the user the option to record a conversation (subject to applicable law). For example, an audio conference call can be recorded. VoIP offers more opportunities to do this, since the cell phone—particularly a mobile phone—is a smart device, unlike a traditional desk phone.

One Specialized App

The Fall 2013 International Association of Chiefs of Police Conference made a mobile app available to its participants. This app helped participants navigate a large physical venue, placed sessions of interest on their personal calendars, and provided other services to facilitate a participant's conference experience. In order to do so, the app requested permissions (of the participants' mobile devices—smartphones) to track users' location and access and modify their calendars and contacts (see Appendix A).

Viewed through a privacy lens, the most serious issue is the vulnerability this app (and others like it) might imply for the senior leadership of thousands of law enforcement agencies and their contacts. What potentially confidential information was on their phones? While we have no reason to suggest that such data were collected, stored, or exploited, the point is the conference organizers' and participants' apparent lack of awareness of the potential to do so. How many participants were aware of what this app was doing, and, if they were, how many would have been comfortable using the app?

Consider a hypothetical scenario in which a crime occurred at the conference. Viewed through a law enforcement lens, would anyone have considered the data collected by this app as potentially helpful to the investigation? What legal processes would have been required to access the data? How many participants were aware of the data this app accessed? How long were these data retained, and for what purpose? Who else was provided with these data?

SOURCE: Analysis of the data access permissions requested by the app. The app was built by Core-Apps, a firm specializing in conferences and expos (Core-Apps, no date).

and services and the data they provide, law enforcement is likely to be unaware of alternative sources of data helpful to an investigation.

It has long been understood that criminals are early adopters of technology (Standage, 1998). Criminal exploitation of mobile technology, apps, and services is no exception. First, privacy-enhancing technologies, such as onion routing (e.g., Tor), are designed to make it difficult to identify the origin of a communication, query, or transaction. Encryption can be used to deny access to communications content or certain transactional details. While there are many societal benefits for privacy-enhancing technologies such as encryption, these technologies can also make it more difficult for law enforcement to access information during a criminal investigation, even with appropriate legal protections. Second, with the large number of apps and services available for mobile devices, law enforcement may be unaware that a particular app or service may have information that is relevant to an investigation. Criminals can exploit the large numbers of apps by moving between similar apps and services or using little-known apps and services to intentionally make their actions more difficult to follow.

Legal Implications

The body of law pertaining to the surveillance of mobile technology is complex and unsettled. While Supreme Court jurisprudence has long held that there is no Fourth Amendment protection for information held by a third party, such as a commercial entity (*Smith v. Maryland*, 442 U.S. 735 (1979)), recent indications suggest that at least some members of the court may consider Fourth Amendment protections appropriate for third party data that reveals particularly intimate information. One Supreme Court justice has suggested a wholesale reexamination of the third-party doctrine, stating that "it may be necessary to reconsider the premise that an individual has no reasonable expectation of privacy in information voluntarily disclosed to third parties" (*United States v. Jones*, 132 S. Ct. 945, 957 (2012)). In the law enforcement context, the debate over third-party data has focused in particular on historical cell phone tower data.[5] This is an evolving area of the

---

[5]   The law in this area is highly uncertain and still developing. Two courts of appeals have determined that the use of cell tower data without a warrant is not unconstitutional. *In re Application of the United States of America for Historical Cell Site Data*, 724 F.3d 600, 615 (5th Cir. 2013), *United States. v. Davis*, 785 F.3d 498 (11th Cir. 2015). However, a magistrate judge from the Eastern District of New York held that "the Fourth Amendment requires the

law, and it is unclear how future courts will decide the issue. However, this legal uncertainty may have a profound effect on decisionmakers today: Law enforcement may not be utilizing cell phone tower data in an optimal way because of the legal uncertainty about whether the data can be lawfully requested.

Legal uncertainties in this area permeate all levels of law enforcement decisionmaking, including the actions of a street-level beat officer. For example, until recently, courts were split on whether law enforcement officers may search the contents of a cell phone obtained when a suspect is arrested.[6] The Supreme Court recently clarified the issue in *Riley v. California*, holding that a warrant is generally required before police may search the contents of a cell phone incident to an arrest.[7] The legal uncertainty due to evolving mobile technology therefore cannot be managed by higher-level decisionmaking; every member of law enforcement must confront it. In the face of these uncertainties, some agencies may not use electronic surveillance as effectively as they could.

One important additional source of legal complexity may be the desire to draw distinctions between the resolution[8] of collected data and the law governing access. Location data are a good illustration of this point. Depending on the source of information—carrier, device,

---

government to obtain a warrant, based on a showing of probable cause on oath or affirmation, in order to secure" the disclosure of cell phone tower information over a period of 58 days. *In the Matter of an Application of the United States of America for an Order Authorizing the Release of Historical Cell-Site Information,* 736 F. Supp. 2d 578, 579 (E.D.N.Y. 2010).

[6] For example, the Ohio Supreme Court held that "the warrantless search of data within a cell phone seized incident to a lawful arrest is prohibited by the Fourth Amendment when the search is unnecessary for the safety of law-enforcement officers and there are no exigent circumstances." *State v. Smith*, 124 Ohio St. 3d 163, 170-171 (Ohio 2009). In contrast, the Fifth Circuit has held that obtaining evidence from a "warrantless, post-arrest search" of the suspect's cell phone did not violate the Fourth Amendment *United States. v. Finley,* 477 F.3d 250, 253 (5th Cir. 2007).

[7] *Riley v. California*, 134 S. Ct. 2473 (2014).

[8] Data resolution refers to the frequency, accuracy, and precision with which the data are collected. For example, two apps may record location information, but one app may record it once per day, accurate to a few feet, while another may record it every five minutes, accurate to a few blocks.

app, or service—location data are collected differently. The accuracy of coordinates and the time at which users were observed, as well as the frequency of the observations, vary significantly.

Furthermore, federal lawmakers have been slow to respond to the privacy issues being raised by the widespread use of mobile devices, apps, and services. The last comprehensive privacy law in the area of communications technology was passed in 1986, and courts have struggled to apply it to emerging technologies. Meanwhile, state lawmakers have and will continue to forge ahead to change state law.[9] Will their approaches converge, or will there be greater diversity of laws and more complexity?

Policy Implications

Policy choices are encoded as law and regulation. Courts interpret the laws and regulations and attempt to resolve ambiguity. Policy choices can change the rules governing law enforcement access to electronic surveillance data, regulate pricing variations for compliance with court orders, regulate the timeliness of compliance with orders, or compel uniform commercial data retention periods. Not all policy choices are public. Corporations have policies that encode their own interpretations of the law and govern how they act upon a law enforcement request.

Policy decisions can reduce uncertainties about electronic surveillance. They can also refine how we meet the needs of public safety and criminal investigations without unacceptably invading the privacy of those using mobile technology or overly burdening commercial

---

[9]   International laws play a role as well. Many of the commercial entities of interest to state and local law enforcement are global firms. To provide a uniform worldwide experience to users, there is pressure to take a "lowest common denominator" approach to compliance with international laws that govern access to data by law enforcement. There is also the pressure to retain stored content in jurisdictions that provide the most favorable terms for commercial use. Thus, international law also exerts an influence on the data that can and will be collected and retained in the future, as well as the jurisdictions that must be considered to access such data.

interests. Such decisions should be informed by empirical information about the use of electronic surveillance, its costs, and its effectiveness.

Goals and Objectives

To define our goals and objectives, we began by summarizing the interests of the various stakeholder groups. This summary is provided in Table 2.1.

Law enforcement officials need a tool to help meet the challenges associated with this complex landscape—something that functions like a "map,"[10] guiding them through the mobile ecosystem and laws governing access to mobile data. At the most basic level, such a tool could increase awareness of available technology and data that may be used in or for criminal purposes. With a better understanding of what data

Table 2.1
Summary of Stakeholder Interests

Stakeholder Groups	Challenges
Commercial entities	Commercial entities would like better-framed and more uniform law enforcement information requests, in order to reduce the burdens of complying with these requests and to better protect the privacy interests of their customers.
Law enforcement	Law enforcement needs to know what information is available within the mobile ecosystem and how to access it quickly and effectively during criminal investigations.
Legal decisionmakers	Legal decisionmakers want greater clarity regarding existing laws and an easier way to identify potential areas of uncertainty.
Policy decisionmakers	Policy decisionmakers want more information about information sharing within the mobile ecosystem in order to craft policies that balance privacy interests and public safety issues.

---

[10] The familiar notion of a map relates concepts such as streets and rivers to geography showing their relationships to one another in a two-dimensional space. We use a map to show how facts about abstract concepts, such as businesses, apps and services, commercially collected data, and electronic surveillance law, relate to one another (without reference to geography). The result is a multidimensional space that can be explored using any of these abstractions as the starting point.

are available and where, the tool could be used to assist investigations, manage costs, and reduce the risk of overlooking relevant law and judicial doctrine. It also could be used to learn about the arguments for and implications of policy changes that govern law enforcement access or regulate commerce. Law enforcement could use this tool to capture and share the latest information about how to work with particular app and service providers to lawfully access data they collect and to better understand what information commercial entities require in an electronic surveillance order, how to convey that order, and how compliance with an order will be achieved. A map of the mobile ecosystem could also convey the complexity of the electronic surveillance landscape to policymakers and could be used to inform policy decisions.

Therefore, our goals in this project are two-fold: (1) to develop a tool that facilitates understanding of electronic surveillance in the mobile ecosystem and (2) to evaluate whether that tool has the potential to promote effective surveillance practice and effective policymaking. Reflecting on the utility of mobile devices, apps, and services in different contexts and for different stakeholders and the desire to create a tool that would facilitate access to that information, we identified the following objectives to guide our tool's development. They define the functional capabilities of our prototype:

1. Create a dynamic encyclopedia of mobile apps and services, the types of data each collects and provides, and the owners.
2. Provide organized information to assist law enforcement in legally and cost-effectively utilizing electronic surveillance of mobile technology.
3. Create a mechanism through which commercial organizations can specify the information they require to respond to court orders, including standards for requesting and responding to a court order.
4. Capture variations in legal requirements associated with electronic surveillance and inform policymaking in electronic surveillance law.
5. Utilize publicly available information wherever possible so that the tool can be updated and expanded.

We also identified secondary objectives that characterize how using the tool could affect electronic surveillance practice and policy:

1. Clarify utilization of the mobile ecosystem for investigatory purposes.
2. Inform the discussion about the interplay between legal surveillance and legitimate privacy concerns.
3. Assist decisionmakers in crafting policies related to surveillance of the mobile ecosystem.
4. Facilitate the sharing of best practices, lessons learned, and investigatory techniques relevant to the mobile ecosystem.
5. Ensure that the information is as up to date and as expansive as possible.

The next chapter describes our approach to developing this tool and how it meets these objectives.

CHAPTER THREE

How MIKE Was Developed

We created the Mobile Information and Knowledge Ecosystem (MIKE) to demonstrate how a map-like tool can be used to help understand the potential avenues for electronic surveillance of mobile technology. We considered other existing maps of mobile technology as possible approaches, but none contained the range of capabilities we envisioned for MIKE. These maps are static and range from non-academic infographics, with limited information, to maps designed for specific applications that capture a narrow set of information and are not generally suited to multiple stakeholder groups.

For example, we reviewed academic work focusing on cataloging groups of firms. However, the surveillance data collected and retained by the firms are not the primary focus of these maps. The MOBILE LUMAscape, shown in Figure 3.1, is an iconic example of this type of map. Developed by LUMA Partners, "LUMAscapes" group together and arrange firms in a logical array from "marketer" to "consumer," color coding each type of entity. The impression one gets from this depiction is the sheer number and complexity of the firms involved in the ecosystem. The depictions have utility in discovering new market segments and representative firms to further investigate, but do not provide specific information on how information is gathered or shared between particular entities.

Figure 3.1
The Mobile LUMAscape Map

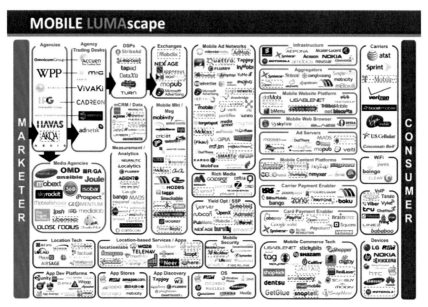

SOURCE: LUMA Partners, "Mobile LUMAscape," 2015. As of October 22, 2015:
http://www.lumapartners.com/lumascapes/mobile-lumascape/
RAND *RR800-3.1*

Data Categories

In contrast, our approach focuses on defining the types of entities involved with mobile technology, the types of data those entities collect, the relationships that can exist between those entities and data types, and the laws governing the interactions between those entities and law enforcement. As such, it combines elements from other mapping approaches with new features relevant to law enforcement practitioners and architects of public policy.

We assume that technology, commercial uses of it, and the body of law governing law enforcement access are in flux and will remain so for the foreseeable future. So we created a dynamic tool in which data could be expanded and refined as users discover new information and existing relationships change. MIKE is designed so that multiple parties can refine and use it for different purposes, as described in Chapter Two. It is based on well-defined categories of information and explicitly defines the relationships between them, making that information available to users of the tool.

The principal categories of information include:

- Commercial entities and their attributes, such as ownership, points of law enforcement contact, and price and timeliness of compliance with court orders
- Products, including mobile apps and mobile operating systems
- Data types and how they are collected and retained, such as the manner of storage, security mechanisms (such as encryption), how long the data are retained, and their accuracy and precision
- Activities that firms or apps engage in and that can be tied to certain legal concepts
- Legal concepts and documents governing law enforcement access to data, e.g., an Electronic Communications Privacy Act 2703(d) court order
- Relationships between all the categories defined above. For example, a firm can be a *subsidiary of* another firm and *own* mobile apps; mobile apps can *collect* and *transmit* data to other firms and *have versions* for certain operating systems; legal concepts are *applicable to* certain data types, jurisdictions, and contexts.

MIKE is dynamic and intended to be used interactively to explore and identify alternative sources of relevant data, as illustrated in Figure 3.2—a screen capture of the list of apps (currently included in our prototype tool) that collect some type of location information at different resolutions.[1] MIKE can then be used to identify the relationships between data sources and laws governing access to them that are relevant to different jurisdictions and contexts—helping to maintain awareness of a complex landscape of apps, services, and law. Figure 3.3, another screen capture from MIKE, provides an example of this—

---

[1] Within our prototype map, *street address* is user account data that may or may not indicate the location of the device owner, while *GPS location*, *latitude and longitude*, and *cell site* refer to the location of the mobile device.

Figure 3.2
Sources of Location Data Known to the MIKE Prototype

Read   Edit   View history ▾   Search

[edit]

Category   Discussion

Category:Location

Data about somebody or something's physical position. Examples include GPS Location data, home addresses, home zip code, and current metropolitan area. Location can be precise or imprecise in both geographic and temporal dimensions.

Create New Data Type

Mobile Applications with Location Data

⬧	Data Context Name	⬧	Data Type	⬧	Encryption	⬧	Resolution ⬧	Retention ⬧
Angry Birds	Angry Birds/Location		GPS Location					
			Wi-Fi Location					Unclear
			IP Address					
Badoo	Badoo/Location		GPS Location				Usage based	Life of account
Badoo	Badoo/Photos and Videos		Photo				Usage based	Life of account
			Video					
Brightest LED Flashlight	Brightest LED Flashlight/Location Data	GPS Location					
DropBox	DropBox/Account Information		Real Name		Entity level encryption	Usage based	Life of account
			Phone Number					
			Email Address					
			Street Address					
DropBox	DropBox/Files		Files		Entity level encryption	Usage based	Life of account
Facebook App	Facebook App/Checkin		GPS Location		No encryption	Usage based	Perpetual
			Post					
			Friends					
Facebook App	Facebook App/Events		Street Address		No encryption	Usage based	Perpetual
			Latitude and Longitude					
			Group Membership					
			Office Holder					

RAND RR800-3.2

Figure 3.3
The Relationship Between a Source of Location Data and the Law Governing Access

Page   Discussion

Read   Edit with form   Edit   View history ▾

▲ Fwalter Talk Preferences Watchlist Contributions Log out

Search   [Go] [Search]

< >

Navigation
Main page
Community portal
Current events
Recent changes
Random page
Help

Toolbox
What links here
Related changes
Upload file
Special pages
Printable version
Permanent link
Browse properties

Foursquare/Radar
‹ Foursquare

Foursquare launched a new feature in October of 2012 called "Radar". At the time, it was only available for iOS devices, but it was planned for Android and other platforms as well. Radar allows continuous location based tracking and is used to inform a user of their proximity to friends, or locations associated with items on their To-do list.

It is highly likely that this information is now being shared with Microsoft in a deal announced Feb 4th, 2014.[1]

Transmitted To	Foursquare Labs Inc., Microsoft
Has Data Type	GPS Location
Encryption Type	
Storage Mode	Remote Storage
Resolution	At intervals
Interval	1 min
Retention	Life of account
References	http://foursquare.com/legal/privacy ⚹ http://blog.foursquare.com/2011/10/13/all-your-burning-questions-about-foursquare-radar/ ⚹
Context Owner	Foursquare

Legal Information

	Required Document		Jurisdiction
ECPA/User Data	⬥	ECPA/2703(d) court order	⬥ United States jurisdiction

[edit]

References

1. ↑ http://www.wired.com/business/2014/02/tracking-war-foursquare-microsoft/ ⚹

Category: Data Context

Facts about "Foursquare/Radar" ⓘ ⁱⁱ

Has data   GPS Location + ⚹

Has resolution interval   6.944444e-4 days (0.0167 hours, 1 minutes, 9.920625e-5 weeks, 2.314813e-5 months, 1.902598e-6 years, 60 seconds) + ⚹

RDF feed ♆

showing the laws governing access to one particular source of location data, Foursquare/Radar.[2] For example, this figure explicitly indicates that a 2703(d) court order is probably required to obtain the location information from Foursquare.

Mapping Variations in Law and Informing Policy

An important attribute of our approach is the ability to capture state-to-state variations in the laws governing law enforcement's access to information generated and stored by mobile technology. Such variations are not necessarily wrong or undesirable, and may reflect well-reasoned policy decisions. However, these variations may cause unintended consequences if they can be opportunistically exploited in a way that either violates privacy expectations or facilitates criminal behavior. By demonstrating the differences between laws in different jurisdictions, we hope to facilitate informed policymaking in this area. For example, a decisionmaker could ask whether a data type, such as location, should be treated uniformly, independent of the commercial purpose for collecting it, the resolution with which it is collected, or the length of time it is stored.

Policymakers and law enforcement share an interest in the consistency of commercial responses to court orders. For example, a U.S. congressman sought to understand pricing variations in responding to court orders (Lichtblau, 2012). Information on the cost of surveillance orders is important to law enforcement—particularly when budgets are constrained. If the same data (e.g., location) could be obtained from multiple sources, then the cost and timeliness of access are important inputs to deciding which source to use. Assuming data are affordable, timely access is important to successfully concluding a criminal investigation. If it takes weeks to obtain a response to an order, and

---

[2] It is important to be clear that our map does not offer legal advice. It simply catalogs laws that the curator deems relevant to lawful access to a particular type of data in a particular context (e.g., a traffic stop, or consent). It serves as a checklist to remind an investigator of the requirements he or she needs to consider in determining how to lawfully access the data from a particular source.

that response leads to subsequent orders that take weeks to satisfy, the momentum of an investigation can be lost. Delays can also have very serious public safety consequences in particularly time-sensitive investigations—e.g., finding an individual who is lost or kidnapped.[3] Even anecdotal evidence pertaining to variations in cost and timing could inform policy choices. Furthermore, if sufficient evidence is collected, it may be possible to analyze the factors underlying variation in cost and timing, which would be of great use to those crafting new policies.

The commercial, technical, and legal relationships described above can be searched and navigated as directed by a stakeholder's goals. New material can be easily added and incorporated in MIKE's web of information. Information can be readily edited, revised, and extended like a wiki—and in fact MIKE is based on the same software as Wikipedia. Relationships between the concepts defined by our tool can be automatically populated based on attributes of the information (e.g., access to specific data types require a 2703(d) court order). Furthermore, MIKE allows the user to trace who added the information presented, and incorporates external references that provide additional detail. But the real power of MIKE is that it captures relationships between the concepts in a format that can be searched.

Sources of Information and Limitations

We populated the MIKE prototype using publicly available information describing more than 40 mobile apps,[4] carriers, device operating systems, and services accessed by those apps. We included legal information from federal sources, six selected states, and the District

---

[3]   Law typically provides exceptions for exigent circumstances, but decisions about what constitutes an exigent circumstance remains a judgment call. We were given as an example the decision (and delay needed) to contact the relative of a lost hiker to give consent to access the last known location of the hiker's mobile device.

[4]   We selected these apps opportunistically based on their popularity, the existence of a privacy policy, and their usefulness for demonstrating potential uses of MIKE.

of Columbia.[5] This information was obtained by reading privacy statements, examining the permissions requested by apps (e.g., access to location information), reviewing publicly available information, and summarizing state and federal law. The tool does not provide legal advice or case management.

---

[5]   We selected states for inclusion based on their influence on electronic surveillance policy, their prior activities in the area, and the existence of law enforcement partners within the state.

CHAPTER FOUR

How MIKE Works

MIKE—the Mobile Information and Knowledge Ecosystem—is a tool developed to enable people to easily explore how information is shared within the mobile ecosystem, and the legal protections in place access to that information. This tool is designed to operate like a map, guiding the user through the entities and information comprising the mobile ecosystem. It can be used by a wide variety of stakeholders, including law enforcement officers, advocates, policymakers, and the general public.

MIKE is based on the same software as Wikipedia, so it is easy to understand and navigate. Because of its familiar layout, we have found that even new users can find what they are looking for. As shown by Figure 4.1, MIKE's homepage includes several different mechanisms to enable the user to find the information he or she seeks: a search bar at the top, quick links that direct the users to specific types of information, and query wizards that can be used for a more refined search.

This software includes specific information about the commercial firms involved in the mobile ecosystem, including the data types they collect, how they can be contacted by law enforcement, and the information they will need in order to identify the targets of information requests. Much like Wikipedia, each commercial firm is described on its own page, with links that enable the user to explore the information provided in more depth. For example, a user who was exploring the page associated with a particular commercial firm would see a table describing the different types of data it collects, and could click on each data type to obtain more information.

Figure 4.1
MIKE's Homepage

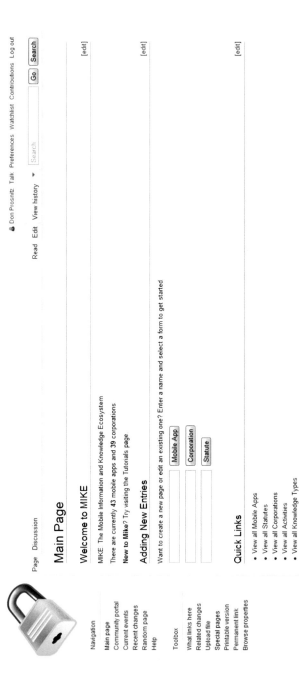

RAND *RR800-4.1*

Just as each commercial firm has its own page, each type of data collected by the commercial firm is described in depth on its own page. Figure 4.2 shows how MIKE describes the account information collected by Google. It provides both technical information (such as the presence and type of encryption) and legal information (such as the legal processes for obtaining the information).

MIKE also contains information about the laws and policies governing law enforcement access to the mobile ecosystem (Figure 4.3). The user can explore specific statutes and cases, investigate how the law differs across different states, and even probe the laws implicated by key policy issues. Wherever possible, MIKE provides direct quotes from the law and a link to the full text, to facilitate further legal research.

MIKE renders its data as familiar web pages with hyperlinks. To do this, MIKE embeds the formalisms of an entity-relationship model into the content of its pages to create a *semantic wiki*. For example, Google is a commercial firm, location is a data type, and a 2703(d) court order is a legal rule—all are examples of entities. The entities are further specified by their relationship to other entities. For example, the data types (an entity) collected by a commercial firm (another entity) are defined by multiple relationships, e.g., location is collected (a relationship) by Google and other commercial firms, and there are legal rules that must be observed to access that data type (a relationship), e.g., a 2703(d) court order.

By using the entity-relationship formalism, it becomes possible to derive standard links between pages and, more importantly, to search based on relationships. For example, the page describing Google will point to a data type describing location, and to the legal rules that must be observed for law enforcement to gain access to location data. These relationships enable complex and useful searches beyond what is possible with a text search of the web pages; for example, finding all of the commercial entities that collect the data type location, or finding all data types that require a 2703(d) court order.

Relationships make it possible for a search to compute a table of links that can be systematically explored by the user. These same formalisms also simplify the task of populating the data in MIKE by replacing handcrafted links between pages with relationships between

Figure 4.2
MIKE's Description of Technical Information

Steven Isley Talk Preferences Watchlist Contributions Log out

Search [ ] Go Search

Page Discussion

Read Edit with form Edit View history ▾

Google Inc./Account Information

‹ Google Inc.

Google keeps unified account information that is shared across all its products and services. This mean that if you know a users pseudonym on one Google product, you can get the information for all other Google products or services that they use

Transmitted To	Google Inc.
Has Data Type	Real Name, Cookie ID, Email Address, Phone Number
Encryption Type	
Storage Mode	Remote Storage
References	http://www.google.com/policies/privacy/ ⟳
Context Owner	Google Inc.

References

Category: Data Context

Facts about "Google Inc./Account Information ⓘ"

Has data   Real Name + ⚲, Cookie ID + ⚲, Email Address + ⚲, and Phone Number + ⚲
Has storage mode   Remote Storage + ⚲
Has support url   http://www.google.com/policies/privacy/ ⟳ + ⚲
Is transmitted to   Google Inc. + ⚲

Legal Information

◆	◆ Required Document ◆
ECPA/Basic Subscriber Information	Administrative Subpoena

[edit]

RDF feed ⚙

Navigation
Main page
Community portal
Current events
Recent changes
Random page
Help

Toolbox
What links here
Related changes
Upload file
Special pages
Printable version
Permanent link
Browse properties

Figure 4.3
MIKE's Description of Legal Information

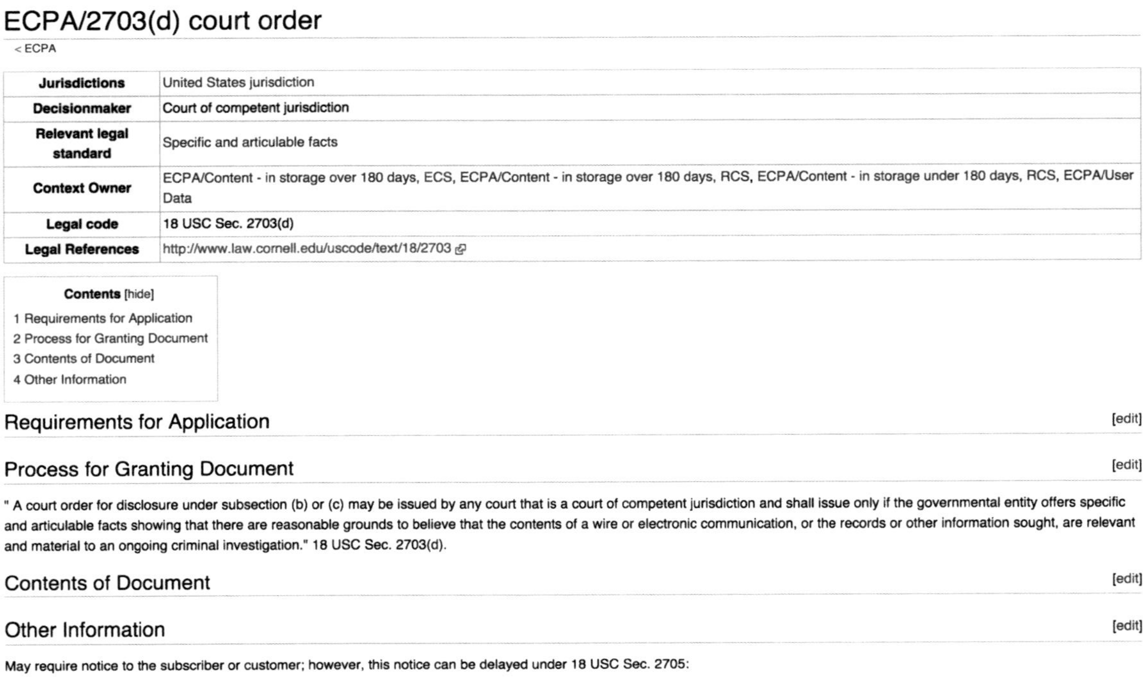

ECPA/2703(d) court order

< ECPA

Jurisdictions	United States jurisdiction
Decisionmaker	Court of competent jurisdiction
Relevant legal standard	Specific and articulable facts
Context Owner	ECPA/Content - in storage over 180 days, ECS, ECPA/Content - in storage over 180 days, RCS, ECPA/Content - in storage under 180 days, RCS, ECPA/User Data
Legal code	18 USC Sec. 2703(d)
Legal References	http://www.law.cornell.edu/uscode/text/18/2703 ⏤

Contents [hide]

1 Requirements for Application
2 Process for Granting Document
3 Contents of Document
4 Other Information

Requirements for Application   [edit]

Process for Granting Document   [edit]

"A court order for disclosure under subsection (b) or (c) may be issued by any court that is a court of competent jurisdiction and shall issue only if the governmental entity offers specific and articulable facts showing that there are reasonable grounds to believe that the contents of a wire or electronic communication, or the records or other information sought, are relevant and material to an ongoing criminal investigation." 18 USC Sec. 2703(d).

Contents of Document   [edit]

Other Information   [edit]

May require notice to the subscriber or customer; however, this notice can be delayed under 18 USC Sec. 2705:

RAND RR800-4.3

entities that enable MIKE to automatically compute additional implied relationships. Thus, MIKE's "secret sauce" is the entities and relationships that it uses to capture, structure, and search the information it is given.

Although we have described several key existing features of MIKE, it should be noted that MIKE's primary strength is its flexibility and robustness to change. Not only can the information contained within MIKE be changed as law and technology develops, but it will also be possible to add additional types of information and references to other resources. As MIKE is adopted, we anticipate that user feedback will help guide the development of additional features as needed.

CHAPTER FIVE

Assessing the Value of MIKE: Stakeholder Reactions

A small number of representatives from three stakeholder groups—the law enforcement community, industry, and policy advocacy groups—participated in demonstrations of MIKE and provided feedback about its structure and potential utility. These conversations generally involved a discussion of the problems MIKE was designed to address, a demonstration of MIKE's capabilities, and then a discussion of the pros and cons of such an approach. However, the specifics of each conversation was generally guided by the interests of the stakeholder representatives and the questions they had regarding MIKE. These meetings also offered an opportunity for open-ended discussions about the scope of the policy problem, but stakeholders were not systematically interviewed or surveyed. Thus, the results may not represent what could be obtained from proper sampling and a rigorous interview protocol. That said, these interactions do offer useful insights into the tool's utility and considerations for further development.

MIKE Is a Useful Aid for Navigating the Mobile Ecosystem

Stakeholders universally reflected on the complexity of the mobile ecosystem and the significant costs associated with navigating the system in an effort to obtain information about mobile devices, apps, and services, and the legal framework governing access to this data.

Law enforcement entities are particularly concerned with the multiplicity of communication pathways now available to criminals, many of which may be unknown to law enforcement or be protected by advanced encryption mechanisms. The costs in both manpower and technology to stay conversant with the rapidly expanding field are also a major concern.

Industry stakeholders are uniformly interested in protecting the privacy of their customers, but they also recognize their responsibility to support law enforcement's legitimate needs. However, the cost in time and money of responding to information requests is not trivial, given the many sources of information and various rules governing access. The ability to streamline the process for requests and improve understanding about what information is in fact needed could considerably lower costs to commercial entities in responding to information requests.

Policy advocates are interested in a way to demonstrate to policymakers the complexity of the mobile ecosystem—its technology, the commercial firms that provide it, and the associated legal framework—in order to facilitate better policy decisions and create clearer rules about when and how law enforcement can access the information collected by commercial firms.

All stakeholder groups consulted viewed MIKE as a potentially useful way to explore the mobile ecosystem and understand the laws regulating law enforcement. Our tool could be used to help law enforcement officers identify new sources of information and point toward new investigatory techniques. It would ensure that law enforcement officers received consistent information about how to utilize the mobile ecosystem, thus minimizing the burden on the companies providing the information. By making it easier to navigate the mobile ecosystem, MIKE could both streamline criminal investigative practices and inform the development of policies governing electronic surveillance.

MIKE Can Serve as a Clearinghouse for Best Practices

Law enforcement is best positioned to evaluate operational parameters of electronic surveillance enacted by individual commercial entities, including the cost, retention period, timeliness of compliance, and difficulty of dealing with individual sources of electronic surveillance data. MIKE can be used to capture, share, and analyze such data. Law enforcement currently (and repetitively) shares this type of information via small community mailing lists because it is valued. If captured in a well-organized tool, the information's validity, timeliness, and availability could be improved with reduced effort. It could also be used to facilitate queries and analyses needed to answer policy questions such as those previously described.

MIKE offers a way to organize and store best practices to aid law enforcement agencies and commercial entities in preparing and responding to information requests. Establishing a shared knowledge base is a real and eminent need and should be a high priority for the law enforcement community. As a shared knowledge base, MIKE would also benefit industry by ensuring that information requests are well formed and that responses are provided according to an industry standard. For policy advocates, MIKE would function as an information-sharing mechanism that could help educate new firms about established ways to respond to law enforcement requests. This is a particularly pressing need as law enforcement officers seek information from new participants providing apps or services, who likely are less accustomed to law enforcement requests than carriers and operating system developers.

There Are Several Possible Ways to Expand MIKE

Given the utility of MIKE as a navigation tool for the mobile ecosystem and a clearinghouse for knowledge sharing and best practices, representatives from all stakeholder groups believe that the prototype should be expanded to include new mobile apps and jurisdictions, updated to reflect the development of new laws and legal decisions, and curated to ensure accuracy. They also see the potential to use these data to objectively inform policy choices. However, not all groups agree on how to prioritize expansions and updates to MIKE. For example, law enforcement officers are primarily concerned with ensuring that popular apps and apps that could be particularly useful to criminal organizations are well represented in MIKE. On the other hand, policy advocates want a broad range of apps represented in MIKE, rather than many instances of apps that fundamentally perform the same functions. From their perspective, a range of apps would help demonstrate to policymakers the complexity and variance of mobile devices, apps and services, and the governing legal frameworks.

Concerns Remain About Who Should Be Able to Access MIKE

While information sharing is viewed as an important tool for improving electronic surveillance, both law enforcement agencies and industry groups are deeply concerned about sharing what they consider to be proprietary and/or sensitive information in a tool such as MIKE. If the general public could obtain information about best practices for requesting and obtaining information from mobile applications and services, it may be possible for criminal organizations and individuals to adapt their communication habits in order to render these best practices obsolete and ineffective. While transparency can facilitate the development of electronic surveillance policy, certain types of public disclosure could limit the effectiveness of investigative techniques and the ability of commercial firms to respond effectively to law enforcement requests without serving any meaningful oversight function or providing any benefit to society. Furthermore, commercial companies are concerned that, if the information were available for comparative academic studies, individual companies could be viewed as either unnecessarily hindering law enforcement or as being unduly friendly to law enforcement.

   While these concerns are justified, it should be possible to provide some public access to MIKE without threatening law enforcement's ability to conduct effective investigations or industry's ability to effectively respond to them. One industry stakeholder suggested making a version of MIKE without proprietary law enforcement information available to the public so that it could be used as a tool for policymaking and public education. A limited, public-access version of MIKE would provide policy advocates with a helpful tool to demonstrate policy issues arising in the mobile ecosystem. This approach, however, is not without risk. If a limited version of MIKE is not comprehensive, the absence of certain applications and services in and of itself could convey useful information to criminals.

In general, organizations voiced similar concerns about electronic surveillance, whether they were from law enforcement, industry, or policy advocacy. The important policy determination is not whether society should value privacy or public safety more highly, but rather how to simultaneously provide meaningful privacy protections and facilitate law enforcement investigations. While stakeholder groups may disagree as to the optimal tradeoff between privacy and public safety, they all agree that a compromise is necessary and desirable.

CHAPTER SIX

Sustaining MIKE

One of the biggest challenges in moving from prototype to full implementation of a mobile ecosystem tool is ensuring that the information contained within it is relevant, accurate, and up-to-date. Stakeholders who evaluated MIKE saw potential value, but consistently asked about plans for how it will be sustained. We identified three non-mutually-exclusive alternatives:

- Allow stakeholders to create and refine the data, similar to Wikipedia's approach.
- House the tool in a National Institute of Justice or other federal program.
- Assign the responsibility to a non-profit entity affiliated with law enforcement.

Systematically analyzing these alternatives was beyond the scope of our current study. However, we can highlight some of the issues that any approach needs to consider.

It is important to be clear about *roles and responsibilities.* Separating the roles and responsibilities for access control, operation, curating, and analysis could be useful in managing trust relationships between stakeholders. While law enforcement and public advocacy groups could both use a map of the mobile ecosystem, neither is inclined to collaborate with the other to construct it.[1] Some types of knowledge may need

---

[1]   One officer flatly stated that if public policy advocates had access to the same system they used, law enforcement organizations would not use it—period—regardless of any restrictions placed on various groups.

to be restricted to one constituency. For example, the law enforcement community needs to be able to share its capabilities and discuss its vulnerabilities, but does not want them inadvertently disclosed.

Partitioning the information and controlling access could facilitate more collaboration. Partitioning the tool's information to separate information useful to all stakeholders from that which is useful to a particular stakeholder would be helpful. Full or partial access to the system would be gated based on a user's affiliation. For example, some types of knowledge may need to be available to multiple constituencies, but tailored to each community. Both law enforcement and policy stakeholders benefit from knowing the types of data collected by commercial entities. However, it is important to law enforcement to know the points of contact in those commercial entities for surveillance orders, and to share advice about how to best work with specific firms. Neither law enforcement nor the commercial entities would like this kind of information to be shared outside the police community.

Curating is necessary to assure the quality of the information in the tool. Curating is also necessary to revise and refine the dimensions of the tool, as users identify potential improvements and expansions. A curator could also can provide independent analysis (i.e., unaligned with any stakeholder) of the tool's content that could be used to inform policy debates.

Next Steps

Our approach appears to have value and be worthy of continued development. The next step in that development process would be to move from a prototype to a pilot. A pilot of our tool should have several objectives:

1. Further refine the mapping concepts. MIKE would benefit from more-intuitive (to the user) names for the organizing concepts, improved layouts of the map pages, and enhanced visualization tools.

2. Demonstrate and assess a refined security model where access to content is limited by user class.

3. Engage with a larger and more diverse audience to use the tool and assess its value. An improved version of MIKE, capable of supporting more-comprehensive testing by users, needs to be created and piloted with a small number of stakeholder organizations.

4. Inform an analysis of alternatives for sustaining the tool, considering the alternatives described in this report and others that might be identified.

5. Explore more-efficient means for populating the tool including automated methods.

In addition, a broader pilot offers an opportunity to expand the content and capabilities of the map. Individuals that used the MIKE prototype identified a number of concepts that would be useful additions to the tool:

- guidance and training functions, e.g., how to conduct electronic surveillance when a suspect's mobile device is unknown/unavailable to law enforcement versus a forensic analysis when a phone of a victim or suspect is available[2]
- reported response times and costs for a particular commercial entity to comply with a court order
- configurations of wiring harnesses used by forensic tools organized by phone manufacturer, operating system, and model
- points of contact for other law enforcement organizations that have successfully obtained information gathered by an app.

---

[2] Using information culled from companies' published privacy policies, we constructed a hypothetical use case showing how MIKE might be used under these circumstances in the forthcoming companion volume to this report, *A Guide to the Structure and Intended Use of MIKE.*

APPENDIX A
Permissions Enabled by the Core-Apps Product

Core-Apps provided the mobile device app distributed at the October 2013 International Association of Chiefs of Police meeting. This app requested a large number of permissions from the user's smartphone. Table A.1. contains the full app permissions list that we obtained by examining the operating system permissions settings after the app was installed on one of our phones.

Table A.1
Core-App Permissions

Information Type	Permissions Requested
Social information	Modify your contacts
	Read your contacts
	Read call log
	Write call log
Personal information	Read calendar events plus confidential information
	Add or modify calendar events and send email to guests without owner's knowledge
Location information	Precise location (GPS and network-based)
	Approximate locations (network-based)
Network communication	View network connections
	Receive data from the Internet
	Full network access
	View Wi-Fi connections
	Connect and disconnect from Wi-Fi
Phone calls	Read phone status and identify

Table A.1—continued

Information Type	Permissions Requested
Storage	Modify or delete the contents of USB storage
Camera	Take pictures and videos
Accounts	Find accounts on the device
System tools	Test access to protected storage
Affects battery	Control flashlight
	Prevent device from sleeping
	Control vibration
Applications information	Run at startup

NOTE: Throughout this project, the permissions requested by each app were determined by reading privacy statements published by each company, examining privacy permissions, and opportunistically reviewing statements made by the leadership of various app manufacturers. For purposes of this work, we did not differentiate between "opt-in" and "opt-out" permissions; however, future research could address this complexity.

Real-Time Auctions

Real-time auctions deliver targeted advertising to an individual based on his or her use of a mobile device. Figure B.1 provides a notional description of how an ad is placed on a web page. The types of commercial entities involved in delivering the ad are organized into four groups: supply, auction, demand, and data.

Figure B.1
Real-Time Advertising Auctions

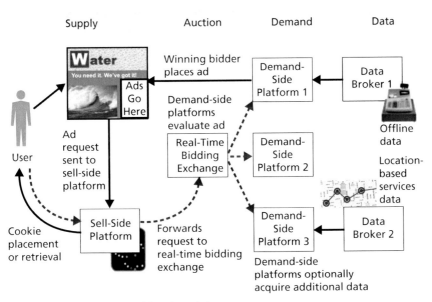

NOTE: This is actually a simplification of the process.

RAND RR800-B.1

Sell-side platforms are used to broker the sale of an advertisement to a user. In this example, the user is viewing the fictional "Water" homepage (upper left hand corner of the figure). The landing page of the user sends a request to the sell-side platform requesting an ad to display on the page. The sell side platform sends a request to a *real-time bidding* exchange (center of the figure) that brokers an auction among multiple *demand-side platforms*—the entities that want to deliver an ad, such as a car ad, to that user. The information provided to the bidders includes information about the user and the user's Internet activities derived from the Universal Resource Locater referenced, cookies, location, and other information.

Demand-side platforms can optionally contract for additional data about the user from *data brokers* (right side of the diagram) before they decide how much to bid for the right to present the ad to the user's "Water" page. Data brokers typically collect information about personal histories, such as residences owned, cars purchased, estimate income and credit scores, or provide location-based information. To use a data broker, the demand-side platform needs to be able to sufficiently "identify" the user to request information about that user (or user's cohort). Identification is accomplished through information wittingly and unwittingly provided by the user and his or her mobile device, apps, and services used.

The demand-side platform that wins the auction delivers the ad, in real-time, to the user's landing page, and reimburses the sell-side platform for the auction price.

References

Camenisch, Jan, and Anna Lysyanskaya, "A Formal Treatment of Onion Routing," *Advances in Cryptology*, Vol. 3621, 2005, pp. 169–187.

Caproni, Valerie, "Going Dark: Lawful Electronic Surveillance in the Face of New Technologies," testimony before the U.S. House of Representatives Committee on the Judiciary, Subcommittee on Crime, Terrorism, and Homeland Security, February 17, 2011.

Chacos, Brad, "Usage for Tor Doubles in Wake of Secure Email Shutdown, Arrival of the PirateBrowser," *PCWorld*, August 28, 2013. As of October 20, 2015: http://www.pcworld.com/article/2047658/usage-for-tor-doubles-in-wake-of-secure-email-shutdowns-arrival-of-the-piratebrowser.html

Cocotas, Alex, "2013—The Year Ahead in Mobile," slide deck, *Business Insider*, January 30, 2013. As of October 20, 2015: http://www.businessinsider.com/2013--the-year-ahead-in-mobile-slide-deck-2013-12?op=1

Comey, James B., "Going Dark: Are Technology, Privacy, and Public Safety on a Collision Course?" remarks to the Brookings Institution, October 16, 2014. As of October 20, 2015: http://www.brookings.edu/events/2014/10/16-going-dark-technology-privacy-comey-fbi

Core-Apps, homepage, no date. As of November 9, 2015: http://www.core-apps.com/

CTIA—The Wireless Association, "Background on CTIA's Semi-Annual Wireless Industry Survey," 2013. As of October 20, 2015: http://files.ctia.org/pdf/CTIA_Survey_YE_2012_Graphics-FINAL.pdf

de Montjoye, Yves-Alexandre, César A. Hidalgo, Michel Verleysen, and Vincent D. Blondel, "Unique in the Crowd: The Privacy Bounds of Human Mobility," *Scientific Reports*, Vol. 3., No, 1376, March 25, 2013. As of October 20, 2015: http://dx.doi.org/10.1038/srep01376

Farivar, Cyrus, "Tor Usage Doubles in Under a Week, and No One Knows Why," *Arstechnica*, August 29, 2013. As of October 20, 2015:
http://arstechnica.com/security/2013/08/
tor-usage-doubles-in-under-a-week-and-no-one-knows-why/

Federal Communications Commission, *Trends in Telephone Service*, Washington, D.C., September 2010.

Google, Google Transparency Reports, various years. As of November 17, 2015:
https://www.google.com/transparencyreport/

In re Application of the United States of America for Historical Cell Site Data, 724 F.3d 600 (5th Cir. 2013).

In the Matter of an Application of the United States of America for an Order Authorizing the Release of Historical Cell-Site Information, 736 F. Supp. 2d 578 (E.D.N.Y. 2010)

Lichtblau, Eric, "Wireless Carriers Who Aid Police Are Asked for Data," *New York Times*, May 2, 2012. As of October 20, 2015:
http://www.nytimes.com/2012/05/03/us/
wireless-carriers-who-aid-police-surveillance-are-asked-for-data.html?_r=0

LUMA Partners, "Mobile LUMAscape," no date. As of October 20 2015:
http://www.lumapartners.com/lumascapes/mobile-lumascape/

McPherson, Aaron, Leslie Hand, and William Stofega, *Technology Selection: Worldwide Mobile Payments 2012–2017 Forecast*, IDC, November 2012.

Meeker, Mary, "Internet Trends 2014: Code Conference," Kleiner Perkins Caufield Byers, May 28, 2014. As of October 20, 2015:
http://www.kpcb.com/blog/2014-internet-trends

National Institutes of Health, "To Whom Does the Privacy Rule Apply and Whom Will It Affect?" last updated February 2, 2007. As of October 20, 2015:
http://privacyruleandresearch.nih.gov/pr_06.asp

Narayanan, Arvind, and Vitaly Shmatikov, "Robust De-Anonymization of Large Sparse Datasets," *IEEE Symposium on Security and Privacy*, 2008.

Riley v. California, 134 S. Ct. 2473 (2014).

Rolfe, Alex, "Alternative Payments to Overtake Credit and Debit Card Payments Globally," Mobile Payments World, May 12, 2014. As of October 20, 2015:
http://www.mobilepaymentsworld.com/
alternative-payments-overtake-credit-debit-card-payments-globally/

Romanosky, Sasha, Martin C. Libicki, Zev Winkelman, and Olesya Tkacheva, *Internet Freedom Software and Illicit Activity: Supporting Human Rights Without Enabling Criminals*, Santa Monica, Calif.: RAND Corporation, RR-1151-DOS, 2015. As of October 20, 2015:
http://www.rand.org/pubs/research_reports/RR1151.html

Rosen, Rebecca J., "When Does Technology Change Enough That the Law Should Too?" *The Atlantic*, December 27, 2013. As of October 20, 2015: http://www.theatlantic.com/technology/archive/2013/12/whendoestechnologychangeenoughthatthelawshouldtoo/282683/

Sharma, Chetan, *2013—The Year in Mobile*, December 23, 2013. As of December 23, 2013: http://chetansharma.com/blog/2013-the-year-in-mobile/

Smith, Aaron, *Nearly Half of American Adults Are Smartphone Owners*, Washington, D.C.: Pew Research Center, March 1, 2012. As of October 20, 2015: http://pewinternet.org/Reports/2012/Smartphone-Update-2012.aspx

Smith v. Maryland, 442 U.S. 735 (1979).

Standage, Tom, *The Victorian Internet: The Remarkable Story of the Telegraph and the Nineteenth Century's On-Line Pioneers*, New York: Walker Publishing Company, Inc., 1998.

State v. Smith, 124 Ohio St. 3d 163 (Ohio 2009).

Statista, "Global Mobile Payment Transaction Volume from 2011 to 2017 (in billion U.S. dollars)," 2014. As of October 20, 2015: http://www.statista.com/statistics/226530/mobile-payment-transaction-volume-forecast/

Sweeney, Latanya, "K-Anonymity: A Model for Protecting Privacy," *International Journal on Uncertainty, Fuzziness and Knowledge-based Systems*, Vol. 10, No. 5, 2002, pp. 557–570.

Swire, Peter, and Kenesa Ahmad, "'Going Dark' Versus a 'Golden Age for Surveillance,'" Center for Democracy and Technology, November 28, 2011. As of October 20, 2015: https://cdt.org/blog/%E2%80%98going-dark%E2%80%99-versus-a-%E2%80%98golden-age-for-surveillance%E2%80%99/

SwitchPay, "Mobile Payment Sales Volume Expected to Exceed 1 Trillion by 2017," summarizing McPherson, Hand, and Stofega (2012), 2014. As of October 20, 2015: http://www.switchpay.com/mobile-payments-sales-volume-trilllion-2017/

Tokson, M. J., "The Content/Envelope Distinction in Internet Surveillance Law," *William & Mary Law Review*, Vol. 50, No. 6, 2009, pp. 2105–2176.

Tor, "Tor Metrics Portal: Users," 2014. As of May 19, 2014: https://metrics.torproject.org/users.html?graph=userstats-relay-country&start=2013-04-01&end=2014-05-19&country=us&events=off#userstats-relay-country

Tor, Tor Project: Anonymity Online, no date. As of October 20, 2015: https://www.torproject.org

Turow, Joseph, *The Daily You: How the New Advertising Industry Is Defining Your Identity and Worth*, New Haven: Yale University Press, 2011.

United States v. Davis, 785 F.3d 498 (11th Cir. 2015).

United States v. Davis, 754 F.3d 1205 (11th Cir. 2015).

United States v. Jones, 132 U.S. 945 (2012).

United States v. Finley, 477 F.3d 250 (5th Cir. 2007).

United States v. Graham, 846 F. Supp. 2d 384 (D. Md. 2012).

United States v. Miller, 425 U.S. 435 (1976).

U.S. Courts, Wiretap Reports, various years. As of November 17, 2015:
http://www.uscourts.gov/statistics-reports/analysis-reports/wiretap-reports

U.S. Department of Health and Human Services, "Entities Covered by the HIPAA Privacy Rule," 2013. As of October 20, 2015:
http://www.hhs.gov/ocr/privacy/hipaa/understanding/training/coveredentities.pdf

Van Hoboken, Joris, "Privacy and Security in the Cloud: Some Realism About Technical Solutions to Transnational Surveillance in the Post-Snowdon Era," *Maine Law Review*, Vol. 66, No. 2, 2014, pp. 488–533.

WhatsApp, homepage, no date. As of November 9, 2015:
http://www.whatsapp.com/